WHY christmas?

Barbara Reaoch

Illustrated by Carol McCarty

Shepherd Press

Why Christmas?
©2012 by Barbara Reaoch
Illustrated by Carol McCarty
Page design, typesetting, cover design by Tobias' Outerwear for Books

ISBN: 9781936908622
ISBN Mobi: 9781936908615
ISBN ePub: 9781936908608

Published by Shepherd Press
P.O. Box 24
Wapwallopen, Pennsylvania 18660

Italics or bold text within Scripture quotations indicate emphasis added by author.

First Printing, 2012
Printed in the United States of America
_____
Library of Congress Cataloging-in-Publication Data

Reaoch, Barbara.
  Why Christmas? / Barbara Reaoch; illustrated by Carol McCarty.
     p. cm.
  ISBN 9781936908622(print book : alk. paper) -- ISBN 9781936908615
(kindle e-book) -- ISBN 9781936908608 (epub e-book)
1. Christmas--Study and teaching. 2. Jesus Christ--Study and teaching. 3.
Families--Religious life. 4. Devotional literature. I. Title.

Get an eBook of *Why Christmas?* at http://www.shepherdpress.com/ebooks

Kindle: ChristmasK
ePub: ChristmasE

JOS 22 21 20 19 18 17 16 15 14 13 12
14 13 12 11 10 9 8 7 6 5 4 3 2 1

Start reading *Why Christmas*? at any time of the year. However, to prepare your family for a meaningful celebration of Christmas, start reading twenty-four days before Christmas day. Stick with a daily plan for family devotions—it will be worth it. Using this devotion before Christmas could be the start of a significant tradition for your family.

How to Use this Devotional

Pray God wants us to know Him and His plan for us through Jesus Christ so He has given us His Word. Start by asking God to help everyone listen and understand what you are about to read.

Read This is the vital part of your devotional time. Engaging with God's Word every day is key for God's children. Read the Scripture references from the Bible to emphasize to your child that God speaks to us through His Word. Shorten or lengthen the Bible reading according to your child's attention span, but do not leave this part out. Even when you have limited time for devotions, read God's Word.

Listen These short comments will help you explain God's Word to your child.

Truth Stating the truth will help your child know what the Scripture teaches about God and His plan.

Discuss Asking good questions stimulates the mind and heart. Engage your child in discussion and encourage application of God's Word to everyday life.

Memorize Children have a great capacity for memorization. Read and memorize one verse (printed in color) each day so that the entire passage is memorized at the end of the week.

Sing The carols were chosen to reinforce the truths of Christ's incarnation. The words for the carols are in the back of this book. Use a Hymnal web site to become familiar with the music. Discussing some of the words and phrases will help to make the carol a meaningful lifelong favorite for your children.

Read: Luke 2:8-16

Listen: Why do we celebrate Christmas? Christmas is fun. Opening gifts is fun. Visiting family and friends is fun. Eating cookies and candy is fun. Is this why we celebrate Christmas? On the first Christmas, the shepherds did not have gifts, friends, and candy. They were tired and hungry from working hard all day. At night there was more work to do. They took turns staying awake to watch the sheep. Were the shepherds excited when they saw the angel? No. The shepherds were afraid. They wondered why the sky was so bright and why God had sent an angel to them. Had they done something wrong? The shepherds were so afraid and there was no place to hide. But when the angel said that Jesus had been born, the shepherds knew this was the best news they had ever heard. God had promised to send the Messiah-King and now He was here. When the angel invited the shepherds to come and meet Jesus, they knew this was an invitation from God. God wanted them to know Jesus.

God wants us to know Jesus, too. This is why He tells us all about Jesus in His Word. The Bible tells us about God's love. It tells us of God's plan to send Jesus into the world. God wants us to know why Jesus was born. At Christmas God invites us to meet Jesus. There is so much to look forward to as Christmas gets closer. Opening gifts, visiting family and eating candy is fun. But Christmas is the celebration of Jesus' birth and Jesus is the greatest gift of all. Christmas is coming. Christmas is the celebration of Jesus' birth.

Truth: Christmas is the celebration of Jesus' birth.

Discuss:

1. What news did the angel give to the shepherds?

2. What do we celebrate at Christmas?

3. What time will you set aside each day to read what the Bible tells us about Christmas?

Memorize: Week 1–Luke 2:1-6

• **Day 1—**Memorize Luke 2:1

[1]***"In those days a decree went out from Caesar Augustus that all the world should be registered."***

• **Discuss:** "Caesar Augustus"

Sing: "Hark! The Herald Angels Sing" (**p.56**)

• **Discuss: "hark" and "herald"**

• **What does "Glory to the newborn king" mean?**

Read: John 1:1-5

Listen: Who is Jesus? Read John 1:1-5 again and this time read "Jesus" instead of "the Word." Jesus is with God and, at the same time, Jesus is God. There is God the Father, and God the Son, and God the Holy Spirit. There is One God who is three Persons. Jesus is not only a man: He is God. In God's power, Jesus created the earth and everything that is in it. Jesus created every star in the sky as well as the mountains and seas. God's Word is powerful and always does whatever God wants (Is. 55:10-11). Jesus is the Word. He is with God and He is God.

When was Jesus born? Your birthday is the celebration of the first day of your life. Jesus' birthday was the first day of His life on earth, but it was not the first day of His life. Jesus has always been alive (Jn. 8:58). Long before Jesus created the stars, sun, moon, and earth, He was alive. Jesus has always been alive and will be alive forever.

Why did Jesus come to live on earth? The Bible says that Jesus came to bring us life and light. That means Jesus came to show us the way to God so that we can live with Him forever. Walking at night by yourself you might get lost if you don't have a flashlight. If you can't see the path you won't know where to go. But you will see the path if a friend, who knows the way and has a flashlight, comes to help. Jesus shows us the way to God. He came to take us out of the darkness of our sin. We celebrate Jesus' birthday because He gives us a gift, which no one else can give - forgiveness of sin and life forever with God.

Truth: Jesus is God.

Discuss:

1. Who is Jesus?

2. When was Jesus born?

3. Why did Jesus come to live on earth?

Memorize: Week 1–Luke 2:1-6

• **Day 2—Memorize Luke 2:2; say verses 1-2**

[1]*"In those days a decree went out from Caesar Augustus that all the world should be registered"*

[2]***"This was the first registration when Quirinius was governor of Syria."***

• **Discuss:: "registration"**

Sing: "Angels from the Realms of Glory " (p. 57)

• **Discuss: *"To the eternal Three in One"***

• **Who are the three Persons in One?**

read: Isaiah 7:14

Listen: How many days are there until Christmas? Before Jesus was born, people knew that He was coming but they did not know when. How did they know Jesus was coming? They listened to the prophets who spoke to the people about God's plan. The prophet Isaiah said that Jesus was going to be "Immanuel". What does Immanuel mean? Immanuel means "God with us." When Jesus was born it was God coming to live with us. The best gift anyone can ever have is to be able to live with God. Living with a loving family is a good gift, but living with God is the greatest gift of all.

A long time ago, Adam and Eve lived with God in a garden called Eden. They were God's first children. God talked with Adam and Eve and took care of them. They were happy living with God until they sinned. Sin is doing what God says not to do. When Adam and Eve sinned they had to stop living with God (Gen. 3:23). To stop living with God was very hard and sad for them. Ever since Adam and Eve disobeyed God, every person is born with the same sin in his or her heart. Each of us wants to be the boss of our own life. We all want to live our way more than God's way. Just like Adam and Eve, we deserve to be punished for our sin. Does this mean that no one can ever live with God? Who can help us?

Only God can help us. Jesus came to live with us. Jesus is Immanuel (Mt.1:23). Jesus took the punishment for our sin when He died on the cross. He overcame the power of sin when He came back to life. Jesus came to live with us so that we can live with God forever.

Truth: Jesus is Immanuel, meaning God with us.

Discuss:

1. What is the punishment for sin?

2. Why is life without God hard and sad?

3. How did God help us?

Memorize: Week 1–Luke 2:1-6

• **Day 3—Memorize Luke 2:3; say verses 1-3**

¹In those days a decree went out from Caesar Augustus that all the world should be registered. ² This was the first registration when Quirinius was governor of Syria ³***"And all went to be registered, each to his own town."***

• **Discuss: "register"**

Sing: "O Little Town of Bethlehem " (p. 58)

• **Discuss: *"Come with us, abide with us, our Lord Emmanuel"***

• **What does it mean that Jesus abides with us?**

Listen: Where was Jesus before He was born? Jesus was with His Father in heaven before He came to the earth. Jesus loved being with His Father (Jn. 17:5). Heaven is so beautiful. The streets are not dirty or rough; they are made of pure gold. The gate is not wooden or worn; it is made of precious pearls. Down the middle of the street runs a river that is not ever muddy; it is crystal clear (Rev. 22:1). There is no need to turn on any lights in heaven because the brightness of God and the glory of Jesus are shining all the time (Rev. 21:23).

In heaven God the Father sits on the throne and Jesus is right by His side (Eph. 1:20-23). The angels in heaven love God and Jesus. They worship God and Jesus all the time and say, "Holy, holy, holy is the Lord God Almighty, who was, and is, and is to come" (Rev. 4:8).

Was it hard for Jesus to leave such a beautiful home to come to earth? The Bible tells us that after Jesus grew up to be a man, He did not have a home or a bed (Mt. 8:20). Not many people loved Him. Not many people believed that He was God (Jn. 1:11-12). Did Jesus ever think it would be better to stay with His Father instead of coming to live with us? No. Jesus did not cling to His Father when it was time to come to earth. Jesus left His beautiful home because He wanted to do what God had planned for Him (John 6:38). God's plan was to give us the best gift of all. God wanted us to be able to live with Him forever. God planned for Jesus to take the punishment for our sin so that we could live with God forever.

Truth: Jesus wanted to do what God had planned.

Discuss:

1. Where was Jesus before He was born?

2. Why did Jesus leave heaven to come to earth?

3. What was God's plan for Jesus?

Memorize: Week 1– Luke 2:1-6

• **Day 4—Memorize Luke 2:4; say verses 1-4**

¹In those days a decree went out from Caesar Augustus that all the world should be registered. ² This was the first registration when Quirinius was governor of Syria ³"And all went to be registered, each to his own town." **⁴ And Joseph also went up from Galilee, from the town of Nazareth, to Judea, to the city of David, which is called Bethlehem, because he was of the house and lineage of David,**

• **Discuss:** Nazareth, Galilee, Judea, and Bethlehem and locate them on a map.

Sing: "Hark! The Herald Angels Sing" (p. 56)

• **Discuss:** *"lays His glories by"*

• **What did Jesus leave when He came to earth?**

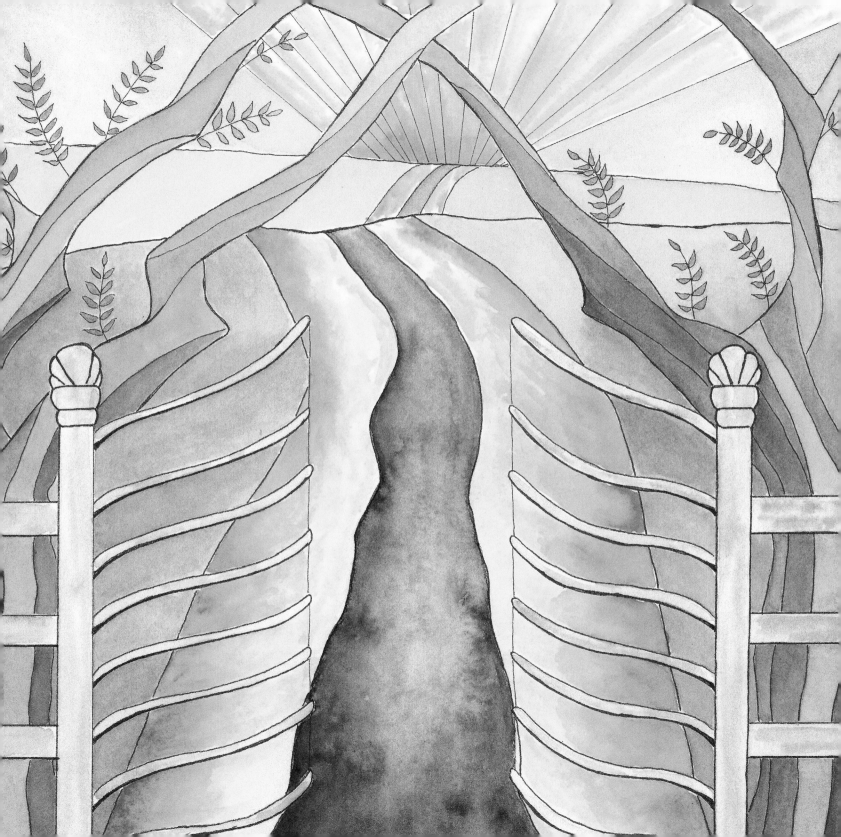

Read: 1 John 4:9–10

Listen: Why did God send Jesus to earth? God sent Jesus to be our atoning sacrifice so we can live with Him forever (Rom. 3:25). The best gift anyone can have is to live with God forever. But sin in our hearts keeps us from coming close to God. God will punish people for their sin. But God loved us so much that He sent Jesus to earth to take our punishment. When Jesus died on the cross, He took the punishment we deserve. When Jesus took our punishment He atoned for our sin. To "atone" means,"to cover." In a bad storm a father will cover his child so that the hail from the storm hits the father and not his child. In the same way Jesus covers us so that the punishment for our sin hits Him and not us.

Long before Jesus was born, God gave the people a special day called the Day of Atonement (Lev. 16). On that day the people did not work or eat. They were sad that their sins kept them from being close to God. They asked God to forgive their lies and unkind thoughts. God loved them so much that He made a way for their sins to be covered. A sacrificial goat took their punishment for sin. The punishment for sin is death. The blood of the sacrifice covered over their sin, and God forgave them.

When Jesus died on the cross, He took the punishment for sin that we deserve (Heb. 2:17). Any boy, girl, Mom or Dad, who trusts in Jesus will have the sin in his or her heart covered. God does not see their sin anymore (Ps. 103:10-13). Jesus died so we can be forgiven and live with God forever.

Truth: God sent Jesus to take our punishment for sin.

Discuss:

1. What keeps us from being close to God?

2. What in our hearts needs to be "covered"?

3. Why did God send Jesus into the world?

Memorize: Week 1–Luke 2:1-6

• Day 5—Memorize Luke 2:5; say verses 1-5

[1]In those days a decree went out from Caesar Augustus that all the world should be registered. [2] This was the first registration when Quirinius was governor of Syria [3]"And all went to be registered, each to his own town." [4] And Joseph also went up from Galilee, from the town of Nazareth, to Judea, to the city of David, which is called Bethlehem, because he was of the house and lineage of David, [5] **He went there to register with Mary, who was pledged to be married to him and was expecting a child.**

• Discuss: *"pledged to be married"*

Sing: "O Little Town of Bethlehem" (p. 58)

• Discuss: *"in this world of sin"*

• Why is the world full of sin?

Listen: Are you sure that Christmas is really coming? You can be sure because Christmas has always come at the same time for many years. But even before the first Christmas, people were sure that Christmas was coming. How did they know about God's promise to send Jesus? God spoke through people called prophets to tell about His plan long before it happened (2 Pet. 1:20-21).

Why did God speak through prophets? God wanted people to know about His plan and His power. Through the prophet Isaiah people learned that Jesus is powerful and the King of all the earth. Jesus is the Prince of Peace. When Jesus is King there will be peace. Other kingdoms come and go, but Jesus' kingdom lasts forever. God wanted people to know that Jesus is God. Jesus is called "Mighty God, and Everlasting Father" because He is God. Jesus is God who came to live on earth.

What else do we learn about God through the prophets? We learn that God knows everything. God knows how many trillions of stars are in the sky and He knows them each by name (Ps. 147:4). God knows each person by name. He knows you because He created you. God knows you so well that He knows how many hairs are on your head (Mt. 10:30). God also knows what will happen in the future. God does not have to guess what will happen. He knows what will happen because He is the One who planned it. God planned the future and He has the power to make sure it will happen just the way He planned. Isaiah says, "The zeal of the Lord Almighty will accomplish it." God has the "zeal" or power to keep His promises and do what He has planned.

Truth: God told people that Jesus was coming long before He was born.

Discuss:

1. How did people know that Jesus was coming?

2. What do we learn about God through the prophets?

3. What is the zeal of God?

Memorize: Week 1–Luke 2:1-6

• Day 6—Memorize Luke 2:6; say verses 1-6

¹In those days a decree went out from Caesar Augustus that all the world should be registered. ² This was the first registration when Quirinius was governor of Syria ³"And all went to be registered, each to his own town." ⁴ And Joseph also went up from Galilee, from the town of Nazareth, to Judea, to the city of David, which is called Bethlehem, because he was of the house and lineage of David, ⁵ He went there to register with Mary, who was pledged to be married to him and was expecting a child. **⁶ And while they were there, the time came for her to give birth.**

• Discuss: "the time came for her to give birth"

Sing: "O Little Town of Bethlehem" (p. 58)

• Discuss: "the hopes and fears of all the years are met in thee tonight"
• What hopes and fears do you think people had before Jesus was born?

read: Galatians 4:4-6

week 1 · DAY 7

Listen: What made Jesus' birthday the right time for Him to come to earth? It was the right time because it was the day God had chosen from the beginning of time. After God chose the day, He got the whole world ready for the time when Jesus would come to live on earth. Jesus came at the exact time God had planned.

Jesus left heaven so that we could have a way to be in God's family and live with Him forever. Living with God forever is the best gift that we can ever have. God is the most powerful Person in the universe, but he lets us come close and talk to Him like a child talks with his father. A child calls out, "Daddy, I need help" when he is afraid. And God lets his children call to him whenever they are afraid or need help.

What did Jesus do so we can call God our Father? Jesus redeemed us. To be redeemed is to be set free from sin. Why do we need to be set free from sin? Sin is powerful. Just like a prisoner cannot get out of jail, we cannot get away from sin. But Jesus is more powerful than sin. He is strong enough to open the jail door and set us free from sin's power. What are we set free to do? We are set free to love God with all our heart. We are set free to live the way God says to live. Sin does not control a child of God. God's child is free to become more and more like Jesus. God's children can call to Him for help (Heb. 2:14-18). You can call out to God and Jesus will give you the power to say "No" to sin.

Truth: Jesus redeems those who put their trust in Him.

Discuss:

1. What does it mean to be God's child?

2. What did Jesus have to do so that you can call God your Father?

3. What are you set free to do?

Memorize: Review Luke 2:1-6

• Day 7—Summarize verses 1-6 in your own words.

¹In those days a decree went out from Caesar Augustus that all the world should be registered. ² This was the first registration when Quirinius was governor of Syria ³"And all went to be registered, each to his own town." ⁴ And Joseph also went up from Galilee, from the town of Nazareth, to Judea, to the city of David, which is called Bethlehem, because he was of the house and lineage of David, ⁵ He went there to register with Mary, who was pledged to be married to him and was expecting a child. ⁶ And while they were there, the time came for her to give birth.

Sing: "Silent Night, Holy Night" (p. 59)

• Discuss: "with the dawn of redeeming grace"

• Why do we need redeeming grace?

18 · week 1 Day 7   WHY CHRISTMAS?

Listen: How did people know that Jesus was the Messiah-King God had promised to send? They knew because of what the prophets had told them. Long before Jesus was born, God told the people that Jesus was going to come from the family of King David (2 Sam. 7:13-14).

Who was King David? David was the youngest son of a man named Jesse. His family lived in Bethlehem. As a boy, David took care of the sheep. David played the harp and loved to sing praises to God (2 Sam. 23:1). One day David heard about a nine-foot giant named Goliath who was saying bad things about God. David was only a boy but he knew that God would help him kill the giant (1 Sam. 17). God chose David to become the king of His people (1 Sam. 16:1-13). God told David that one day the Messiah would come from his family line. David was a great king but the Messiah would be greater and His kingdom would last forever. David was not righteous but the Messiah would be righteous. Jesus is the righteous Branch in the family tree of King David.

What does it mean to be righteous? It means to do everything right and never sin. What does it mean that Jesus is "the Lord our Righteousness?" It means that Jesus kept all of God's commands all the time. He loved God with all of His heart, soul, mind, and strength all the time. He loved us before we loved Him. Jesus is the only one on earth who never sinned (Heb. 1:8-9). It also means that God gives Jesus' righteousness to anyone who puts their trust in Him (1 Cor. 5:21). When God looks at a boy or girl who trusts in Jesus, He does not see their sin anymore – He sees the righteousness of Jesus (Rom. 4: 5-8).

Truth: Jesus is the Messiah-King God promised to send.

Discuss:

1. How did people know that Jesus was the Messiah-King God promised to send?

2. What does it mean to be righteous?

3. What does it mean that Jesus is the Lord our Righteousness?

Memorize: Week 2 - Luke 2:7-12
• **Day 8—Memorize Luke 2:7; say verses 1-7**

*6 And while they were there, the time came for her to give birth. 7 **And she gave birth to her firstborn son and wrapped him in swaddling cloths and laid him in a manger, because there was no place for them in the inn.***

• **Discuss: "manger"**

Sing: "Hark! The Herald Angels Sing" (p. 56)

• **Discuss: "Hail the Son of Righteousness"**

• **What does it mean to "hail" Jesus as the Son of Righteousness?**

Listen: Where did the prophet say Jesus would be born? God told the prophet Micah that Jesus would be born in Bethlehem. Bethlehem was a small town where shepherds watched their sheep. Why did God choose the small town of Bethlehem as the town for the Messiah-King to be born? Long before Jesus was born, God told the people that Jesus would come from the family line of King David (2 Sam. 7:13-14). God chose Bethlehem because He wanted Jesus to be born in the same town where King David lived many years ago.

Before David was King of Israel, he was a shepherd caring for his sheep in Bethlehem (1 Sam. 16:1). David was a good shepherd. He led the sheep to grass to eat and water to drink. He knew each sheep by name and when David called, the sheep knew his voice. When a wolf tried to attack his sheep, David did not run away. He fought the wolf and was willing to die to keep the sheep safe.

David was a good shepherd, but Jesus is the Good Shepherd. Jesus calls us His sheep. Jesus knows each of His sheep by name. Jesus knows us and we can know Him by listening to Him. We listen to Jesus when we read the Bible which is His Word to us. As you know a good friend just by hearing his or her voice, you will learn to know Jesus by reading the Bible. Jesus is the Good Shepherd who leads us to God. Jesus was willing to die to set us free from sin and make us God's children (Jn. 10:1-18).

Truth: Jesus was born in Bethlehem just as God promised.

Discuss:

1. Where did God say Jesus would be born?

2. Why did God choose Bethlehem?

3. Why is Jesus the Good Shepherd?

Memorize: Week 2–Luke 2:7-12

• **Day 9—Memorize Luke 2:8; say verses 1-8**

⁶ *And while they were there, the time came for her to give birth.* ⁷ *And she gave birth to her firstborn son and wrapped him in swaddling cloths and laid him in a manger, because there was no place for them in the inn.* ⁸***And in the same region there were shepherds out in the field, keeping watch over their flock by night.***

• **Discuss: "keeping watch"**

Sing: "O Little Town of Bethlehem" (p. 58)

• **Discuss: *"Yet in thy dark streets shineth, The everlasting Light".***

• **Why is Jesus called the everlasting Light?**

Listen: How are you getting ready for Christmas? Baking, decorating, and shopping for gifts are some ways that people get ready for Christmas. But God wants us to get ready for Christmas in another way too. God wants us to get ready by believing everything He has told us about Jesus. Long before Jesus was born, God sent prophets to tell us about Him. God also said that He was going to send someone like the prophet Elijah before He sent Jesus. That person would get the people ready to meet Jesus (Is. 40:3-5). That man was John the Baptist.

John's parents were Zechariah and Elizabeth. Zechariah was a priest and one day it was his turn to serve in the temple. He went through the heavy curtain into the Holy Place. Zechariah started to light the incense when suddenly there was an angel in the room with him. Zechariah was so afraid. The angel told him not to be afraid, because something wonderful was going to happen. Zechariah and Elizabeth were going to have a baby. This baby was going to grow up to be like the prophet Elijah (Mt. 11:13-14). Zechariah's son was going to get the people ready to meet God's Son, Jesus.

Was Zechariah happy? No. Zechariah heard this good news, but he did not believe that it was true. Zechariah thought it was impossible. He and Elizabeth were too old to have a baby. Many people are like Zechariah. They do not believe what God says. They hear the good news about Jesus but do not believe it is true. They think it is impossible. But everything God tells us about Jesus in the Bible is true. God wants us to get ready for Christmas by believing what He tells us about Jesus.

Truth: God tells us the truth about Jesus in the Bible.

Discuss:

1. What did God tell us about Jesus long before He came to live on earth?

2. Why did Zechariah doubt what the angel told him?

3. What does God want us to believe?

Memorize: Week 2–Luke 2:7-12
• **Day 9—Memorize Luke 2:9; say verses 1-9**

⁷ And she gave birth to her firstborn son and wrapped him in swaddling cloths and laid him in a manger, because there was no place for them in the inn. ⁸And in the same region there were shepherds out in the field, keeping watch over their flock by night.
*⁹**And an angel of the Lord appeared to them, and the glory of the Lord shone around them, and they were filled with great fear.***

• **Discuss:** "glory of the Lord"

Sing: "Angels, from the Realms of Glory" (p. 57)

• **Discuss: "realms of glory"**

 • **What are realms of glory and where are they?**

Listen: How was Jesus going to come into the world? Would Jesus come into the world as a grown man? No, Jesus was coming into the world as a baby. Who was going to be Jesus' father and who would be His mother? Every baby has a father and a mother. But Jesus would be different from every other baby ever born.

Do you remember Zechariah and Elizabeth? They knew it was impossible for them to have a baby. They had been married a long time and now their bodies were too old. But God made it possible for them to have a baby. A new life began to grow in Elizabeth's body, just as the angel had told Zechariah. The baby was John. Later the angel Gabriel came to a young woman named Mary and told her that she was going to be the mother of Jesus. This was good news because the people had waited a long time for God to send the Messiah-King. But Mary knew that it was not possible for her to have a baby. Mary was a virgin; she did not have a husband. She and Joseph were not married yet. Then Gabriel said that the Holy Spirit would make the life of Jesus begin to grow in Mary. Joseph was not going to be the father of the baby. God was going to begin this new life in Mary. God would be Jesus' Father and Mary would be His mother.

Many things are impossible for people but nothing is too hard for God. Jesus' life began in a way that is different from every other baby ever born. No one except Jesus has ever been both man and God. Jesus is the Messiah-King. He is from the family line of King David. And Jesus is the King of the universe forever.

Truth: Mary is Jesus' mother and God is His Father.

Discuss:

1. Who was the father of John?

2. Who was the father of Jesus?

3. Why is Jesus different from every other baby ever born?

Memorize: Week 2–Luke 2:7-12
• **Day 11—Memorize Luke 2:10; say verses 1-10**

7 And she gave birth to her firstborn son and wrapped him in swaddling cloths and laid him in a manger, because there was no place for them in the inn. 8And in the same region there were shepherds out in the field, keeping watch over their flock by night.
9And an angel of the Lord appeared to them, and the glory of the Lord shone around them, and they were filled with great fear.
*10 **And the angel said to them, "Fear not, for behold, I bring you good news of great joy that will be for all the people.***

• **Discuss:** "good news of great joy"

Sing: "Hark! The Herald Angels Sing" (p. 56)

• **Discuss: "Offspring of the Virgin's womb"**

• **Who is the "Offspring of the Virgin"?**

read: matthew 1:18–25

Listen: Who is Joseph? Joseph was a man who loved God. He was engaged to Mary. But before they were married, Joseph learned that Mary was going to have a baby. Joseph knew that he was not the father of Mary's baby. He thought that they should not get married.

One night while Joseph was sleeping, God sent an angel to give him an important message. The angel told Joseph that he should not be afraid to become Mary's husband. The baby's father was not another man. The baby's father was God. God wanted Jesus to grow up in a family that loved Him and took care of Him. God chose Mary and Joseph to be Jesus' parents.

Why was Joseph to give the name "Jesus" to the baby? Because Jesus would save His people from their sins. Why do we need to be saved from our sins? If we are not saved from our sins, we have to take the punishment for sin ourselves. The punishment for sin is living apart from God forever in a place called hell. How does Jesus save us from hell? A lifeguard saves people from dying by pulling them out of the water and breathing life into their body. Jesus saves people from hell by pulling them out of their punishment for sin. And He breathes God's new life into those He saves. Jesus saves the boy or girl who trusts in Him. They will live with God in heaven forever (Jn. 3:16-18). Joseph believed God and did what God told him.

Truth: God is Jesus' Father.

Discuss:

1. Who is Joseph?

2. Why was Joseph to give the name "Jesus" to the baby?

3. From what do we need to be saved?

Memorize: Week 2–Luke 2:7-12
• **Day 12—Memorize verse 11; say verses 1-11**

7 And she gave birth to her firstborn son and wrapped him in swaddling cloths and laid him in a manger, because there was no place for them in the inn. 8And in the same region there were shepherds out in the field, keeping watch over their flock by night. 9And an angel of the Lord appeared to them, and the glory of the Lord shone around them, and they were filled with great fear. 10 And the angel said to them, "Fear not, for behold, I bring you good news of great joy that will be for all the people. **11 For unto you is born this day in the city of David a Savior, who is Christ the Lord.**

• **Discuss: "Savior"**

Sing: "O Little Town of Bethlehem" (p. 58)

• **Discuss: *"Cast out our sin, and enter in, Be born in us today!"***

• **What does it mean for Jesus to cast out our sin?**

Listen: Who is coming to visit you this Christmas? Mary wanted to visit her cousin Elizabeth. Mary was so happy (Lk. 1:46-47). She believed the truth about God's plan to send Jesus. Mary wanted to share the blessings of God with Elizabeth. When Elizabeth heard Mary's voice, the baby inside her body jumped. What did God's Spirit tell Elizabeth? The Spirit of God told Elizabeth that Mary was the mother of Jesus. This made Elizabeth so happy (Lk. 1:43).

Mary and Elizabeth were so happy that God loved them. The sin in their hearts had made them sad. God is holy and He cannot be close to sin. But God loved them so much that He was sending His Son to take the punishment for their sin. God is loving and kind and forgives those who believe the truth about His Son, Jesus.

What does it mean to believe the truth about God and His Son, Jesus? It means to know that God is holy and loving. It means to understand that His plan was to send His Son, Jesus, for the forgiveness of your sin so you can live with God forever. It means that you receive this truth, just as you would receive the best gift ever. How do you receive this gift? Tell God that you believe the truth about His Son, Jesus. Ask Him to forgive your sins. Then thank God for the new, forever life that He promises (Jn. 3:16). The Holy Spirit will you help you understand God's truth and give you a new heart (Ez. 36:26).

Truth: God's Word is true and those who believe Him are blessed.

Discuss:

1. Why did Mary want to visit Elizabeth?

2. What did Mary and Elizabeth believe?

3. What does it mean to believe the truth about God and His Son Jesus?

Memorize: Week 2–Luke 2:7-12

• **Day 13—Memorize Luke 2:12; say verses 1-12**

*7 And she gave birth to her firstborn son and wrapped him in swaddling cloths and laid him in a manger, because there was no place for them in the inn. 8And in the same region there were shepherds out in the field, keeping watch over their flock by night. 9And an angel of the Lord appeared to them, and the glory of the Lord shone around them, and they were filled with great fear. 10 And the angel said to them, "Fear not, for behold, I bring you good news of great joy that will be for all the people. 11 For unto you is born this day in the city of David a Savior, who is Christ the Lord. 12 **And this will be a sign for you: you will find a baby wrapped in swaddling cloths and lying in a manger."***

• **Discuss: "a sign for you"**

Sing: "Silent Night, Holy Night" (p. 59)

• **Discuss: "holy infant tender and mild"**

• **What does it mean that Jesus was a holy infant?**

Listen: What is your favorite Christmas carol? Christmas carols are songs about Jesus' birth. Mary's song was the first Christmas carol. She sang about how big and great God is. Have you ever looked through a magnifying glass? Have you seen how things can look very big through that magnifying glass? Mary wanted her life to magnify God. She wanted people to know how great God is. She sang about God as her Savior, the Mighty One, Holy, and Merciful. He is able to keep all of His promises.

Why did Mary sing about God as her Savior? Mary knew that she was a person just like everyone else. God was not looking for someone smart, rich, or famous to be the mother of Jesus. God does not choose people because of what they will do for Him. He chooses people because of what He will do for them. Mary knew that she had a sinful nature and needed a Savior, just like all of us (Is. 53:6). God gave to Mary the gift of forgiveness of her sin. This forgiveness came through Jesus. Jesus would be Mary's son and also her Savior.

Why did Mary sing about Abraham? A long time before Jesus was born God spoke to Abraham and promised that the Messiah would come through his family (Gen. 12:2-3). God never forgot His promise. Abraham lived many years before King David, but Abraham and David were in the same family (Mt. 1:2-6). The people waited a long time, but God is faithful and always keeps His promises. Everything happens just as God plans because He has the power to make His plans happen. It was finally the right time for the Messiah-King to come into the world, and God chose Mary to be Jesus' mother.

Truth: God is great and keeps all His promises.

Discuss:

1. Why did Mary want her song to magnify God?

2. Why did Mary sing about God as her Savior?

3. How does God keep His promises?

Memorize: Review Luke 2:1-12

• Day 14— Summarize verses 7-12 in your own words

⁷ And she gave birth to her firstborn son and wrapped him in swaddling cloths and laid him in a manger, because there was no place for them in the inn. ⁸And in the same region there were shepherds out in the field, keeping watch over their flock by night. ⁹And an angel of the Lord appeared to them, and the glory of the Lord shone around them, and they were filled with great fear. ¹⁰ And the angel said to them, "Fear not, for behold, I bring you good news of great joy that will be for all the people. ¹¹ For unto you is born this day in the city of David a Savior, who is Christ the Lord. ¹² And this will be a sign for you: you will find a baby wrapped in swaddling cloths and lying in a manger."

Sing: "Silent Night, Holy Night" (p. 59)

• Discuss: "Jesus, Lord, at Thy birth"

• What does it mean that Jesus was Lord at His birth?

Listen: Why were the people surprised when Zechariah wrote on the tablet, "His name is John"? Something had changed in Zechariah's heart. At first he did not believe the angel's message from God. Then he watched the baby grow in Elizabeth's body and started to believe God. What did Zechariah think when he listened to Elizabeth and Mary talk about God? Did they talk about Isaiah's prophecies that tell about Jesus and John (Is. 40:3-5)? By the time Zechariah wrote John's name on the tablet, his mind and heart had changed.

Zechariah knew about God ever since he was a little boy. Zechariah's parent's probably taught him how to pray and read God's Word. He would have memorized Scripture and tried to obey God. But God showed Zechariah something about his heart on the day that he did not believe the angel's message. Zechariah did not really trust God's Word. Sometimes boys and girls grow up knowing about God. They may know how to pray. They can even memorize Scripture and still not trust God's Word. Sometimes grown-ups go to church and are good to their neighbors but do not trust God's Word. Like Zechariah, people can learn to do good things and yet have hearts that do not trust in God.

What does it mean to trust in God? It means to believe God's Word and want to do whatever He says to do. It means to want to live God's way more than your own way. It means to ask God to help you to turn away from your sin and forgive your sins. What happened to Zechariah? He turned away from his sin and believed what God said. He decided to do whatever God wanted him to do. Zechariah put his trust in God.

Truth: God is trustworthy.

Discuss:

1. Why were the people surprised when Zechariah named his son John?

2. What happened to Zechariah during the months that he could not talk?

3. What does it mean to trust in God?

Memorize: Week 3—Luke 2:13-18

• **Day 15—Memorize Luke 2:13; say verses 1-13**

13 And suddenly there was with the angel a multitude of the heavenly host praising God and saying,
14 "Glory to God in the highest, and on earth peace among those with whom he is pleased.

• **Discuss: "a multitude of the heavenly host"**

Sing: "O Little Town of Bethlehem" (p. 58)

• **Discuss: *"meek souls"***

• **What does it mean that Zechariah had a meek soul when he put his trust in God?**

Listen: As it gets closer to Christmas, are you coming closer to God? Zechariah came close to God when he finally believed God's promise that he and Elizabeth would have a son. After Zechariah trusted in God, his heart was so happy that he started to sing. Jesus was coming just as the prophets had said. He was coming from the family line of David. Jesus was coming to unlock our prison of sin and redeem us. Jesus was coming to be our Savior so we can live with God in heaven forever. God is merciful. That means He forgives and helps us. God is faithful and keeps every promise He makes about Jesus, even as far back as Abraham (Gen. 12:2-3).

Zechariah repented of his sin of doubting God's promise. What does it mean to repent? To repent means to stop going away from God. It means to turn around to go the right way - back to God. Zechariah changed the way he was thinking. He stopped thinking that he was right and God was wrong. Zechariah wanted to do whatever God wanted him to do. God wanted Zechariah to be the father of John the Baptist.

John's work was to get the people ready to meet Jesus. When John grew up, he told people to repent. He told them to get ready to meet Jesus (Mt. 3:1-3). Sometimes people think they are close to God because of the good things they do. Or they think God will love them because they do not do bad things like other people. But God looks at our hearts. John told the people that their hearts were not close to God. They needed to repent and come close to God (Ja. 4:8).

Truth: God forgives everyone who repents.

Discuss:

1. What did Zechariah want to sing about?

2. What did John tell the people?

3. What does it mean to repent?

Memorize: Week 3–Luke 2:13-18

- **Day 16—Memorize Luke 2:14; say verses 1-14**

[13] *And suddenly there was with the angel a multitude of the heavenly host praising God and saying,*
[14] *"Glory to God in the highest, and on earth peace among those with whom he is pleased.*

- **Discuss: "peace among those with whom he is pleased"**

Sing: "Hark! The Herald Angels Sing" (p. 56)

- **Discuss: "God and sinners reconciled"**

- **Why do God and sinners need to be reconciled?**

Listen: Do you remember the name of the town where Jesus was born? God said Jesus would be born in Bethlehem. Do you remember why Jesus was born in Bethlehem? Jesus would be from King David's family line. King David's hometown was Bethlehem. People knew the Messiah-King would be born in Bethlehem (Mt. 2:5). Mary and Joseph lived in Nazareth. Nazareth is far away from Bethlehem. How could Jesus be born in Bethlehem when Mary and Joseph lived so far away? Nothing is too hard for God.

At the time of Jesus' birth, Caesar Augustus was the ruler of Rome. He ruled over Bethlehem and Nazareth too. Caesar Augustus thought it was a good idea to count every person under his rule. He wanted to know how many people should give him tax money. But God had another reason for Caesar Augustus to count all the people (Prov. 16:9). God wanted Mary and Joseph to go from Nazareth to Bethlehem. All the families had to go to the hometown of their family to be counted. Joseph was from the family of King David (Lk. 1:27). This meant their hometown was Bethlehem.

It was a long way for Mary and Joseph to travel from Nazareth. As Mary and Joseph traveled did they talk about Micah's prophecy that Jesus would be born in Bethlehem? Were they amazed at God's way of getting them there? God gave Mary and Joseph the courage to do His will. God's plans always happen just the way He says. Sometimes it seems like rulers are in control, but God is the One in control. When everything was just right, God sent His Son (Gal. 4:4-5). Jesus left heaven and came to live on earth (Phil. 2:7). That night in Bethlehem, Jesus, the Prince of Peace was born (Isa. 9:6).

Truth: God's plans always happen.

Discuss:

1. Who was Caesar Augustus?

2. How did God get Mary and Joseph to Bethlehem?

3. What does it mean that God is in control?

Memorize: Week 3–Luke 2:13-18
• **Day 17—Memorize Luke 2:15; say verses 1-15**

*13 And suddenly there was with the angel a multitude of the heavenly host praising God and saying, 14 "Glory to God in the highest, and on earth peace among those with whom he is pleased. 15 **When the angels went away from them into heaven, the shepherds said to one another, "Let us go over to Bethlehem and see this thing that has happened, which the Lord has made known to us."***

• **Discuss: *"the Lord has made known to us"***

Sing: "Silent Night, Holy Night" (p. 59)

• **Discuss: *"Heavenly hosts sing alleluia"***

• **What does it mean to sing alleluia to Jesus?**

Listen: Angels love God and worship Him in heaven all the time. Thousands and thousands of angels are all around God's throne praising Him for who He is (Rev. 5:11-12). The angels praise God because He is Holy (Rev. 4:8). God has never sinned and He cannot get close to sin. Angels know that God is worthy to be praised by all the people He has created (Rev. 4:11). But we cannot get close to God because of the sin in our hearts. What would God do to change this? How would we ever have peace with God? All through the years the angels watched as God's plan to send a Savior became known (1 Pet. 1:12).

God gave angels the special job of telling people that Jesus was coming to earth. Do you remember that an angel told Mary that she was going to be Jesus' mother? Do you remember how the angel came to Joseph to say that Mary should be his wife? Then on the night that Jesus was born, God sent an angel to tell the shepherds. The brightness of God was all around the angel. To the shepherds it may have seemed like they were looking at the sun. The angel gave them the best news that anyone had ever heard – the Savior had been born, just as God had promised long ago.

Suddenly the angels in heaven could not hold back their joy any longer. Thousands and thousands of angels burst through the dark sky to praise God for sending Jesus (Heb. 1:6). This was more beautiful than a flash of lightning or the colorful northern lights. Angels are God's messengers but they are not to be praised. God is the only One to be praised for His plan to send Jesus. Jesus is the Savior God sent so that we can have peace with Him (Heb. 1:7-9).

Truth: God made a way for people to have peace with Him through Jesus.

Discuss:

1. What do the angels in heaven do?

2. What did the angels tell the shepherds about God's plan?

3. For what will you praise God?

Memorize: Week 3–Luke 2:13-18
• **Day 18— Memorize Luke 2:16; say verses 1-16**

13 And suddenly there was with the angel a multitude of the heavenly host praising God and saying,
*14 "Glory to God in the highest, and on earth peace among those with whom he is pleased. 15 When the angels went away from them into heaven, the shepherds said to one another, "Let us go over to Bethlehem and see this thing that has happened, which the Lord has made known to us." 16 **And they went with haste and found Mary and Joseph, and the baby lying in a manger.***

• **Discuss: What does it mean that the shepherds "went with haste?"**

Sing: "Silent Night, Holy Night" (p. 59)

• **Discuss: *"shepherds quake at the sight"***

• **What does it mean that the shepherds quaked?**

Read: Luke 2:15-20

Listen: Did the shepherds wonder why the angels came to them? Why were they the first ones to hear of Jesus' birth? Shepherds were used to being the last ones to hear important news. They lived out in the hill country far from the city. Most people did not like shepherds because they were poor. They did the work that no one else wanted to do. In those days if a king visited a city, he would not go to see the shepherds. Yet when God's King, Jesus, was born, the shepherds were the first people to hear the good news. Jesus is not like any other king.

God loved the shepherds and wanted them to know the good news that Jesus was born to save them from their sins. God does not love people just because they are strong or smart or have a lot of money. God does not love someone when they can play the piano better than anyone else or get more soccer goals than anyone else on the team. It is not when someone does more work at church than anyone else, that God loves them. God does not look at what we do, He looks at our heart. Jesus said we must be poor in heart (Mt. 5:3). Does this mean we must have a heart that is sick? No, it means that I know I do not deserve God's love. It means I know that I have sinned and cannot do anything to make God love me. So when I know that God is inviting me to come to Jesus, I am very happy.

When the shepherds got the invitation to meet Jesus, they did not wait. They hurried to see Him. They were so happy to meet Jesus. The person who is "poor in heart" knows that God's love is a great gift.

Truth: God invites us to come and meet Jesus.

Discuss:

1. Why did God send an invitation to the shepherds to come and meet Jesus?

2. What can you do to make God love you?

3. What does it mean to be "poor in heart"?

Memorize: Week 3–Luke 2:13-18
- **Day 19—Memorize Luke 2:17; say verses 1-17**

[13] And suddenly there was with the angel a multitude of the heavenly host praising God and saying, [14] "Glory to God in the highest, and on earth peace among those with whom he is pleased. [15] When the angels went away from them into heaven, the shepherds said to one another, "Let us go over to Bethlehem and see this thing that has happened, which the Lord has made known to us." [16] And they went with haste and found Mary and Joseph, and the baby lying in a manger. [17] ***And when they saw it, they made known the saying that had been told them concerning this child.***

- **Discuss: "they made known"**

Sing: "Angels, From the Realms of Glory" (p. 57)

- **Discuss "God with man is now residing"**

- **What does it mean to reside?**

Listen: Does it feel like a long time to wait until Christmas? It is not easy to wait for something that we want. Simeon waited a long time to see Jesus. The Holy Spirit told Simeon he would not die before he saw Jesus. Day after day he went to the temple to pray and wait for Jesus to come. Finally the day came when Mary and Joseph brought Jesus to the temple. Jesus was only eight days old, but Simeon knew that He was the Messiah-King. Simeon was so happy that he started to sing to God. How did Simeon know so much about Jesus? Simeon already knew of Jesus because he read God's Word.

What did Simeon know about Jesus? He knew that Jesus would be the Savior for anyone who asks. It does not matter if they are Jews or Gentiles. God chose the Jewish people to tell the world about Him. The Jews tried to obey God's law. The Gentiles were people who did not know about God. They did not try to obey God. They did not know that sin keeps us from coming close to God. But God sent Jesus to be the Savior of the Jews and Gentiles. God forgives anyone who asks for forgiveness. Jesus came for people of every nation, and language. God does not have favorites (Rev. 7:9).

What else did Simeon know about Jesus? He knew that many people would not believe in Jesus. People who do not trust in Jesus will never get to live close to God. They will live apart from God forever, in a place called hell. Simeon was sad to think that some people would not trust in Jesus. But he praised God for sending Jesus. Anyone who trusts in Jesus will live with God in heaven forever.

Truth: God forgives anyone who trusts in Jesus.

Discuss:

1. How did Simeon know so much about Jesus?

2. What did Simeon know about Jesus?

3. What did Simeon know about people who believe in Jesus?

Memorize: Week 3–Luke 2:13-18
• **Day 20—Memorize Luke 2:18; say verses 1-18**

*¹³ And suddenly there was with the angel a multitude of the heavenly host praising God and saying, ¹⁴ "Glory to God in the highest, and on earth peace among those with whom he is pleased. ¹⁵ When the angels went away from them into heaven, the shepherds said to one another, "Let us go over to Bethlehem and see this thing that has happened, which the Lord has made known to us." ¹⁶ And they went with haste and found Mary and Joseph, and the baby lying in a manger. ¹⁷ And when they saw it, they made known the saying that had been told them concerning this child. ¹⁸ **And all who heard it wondered at what the shepherds told them.***

• **Discuss: "all who heard it wondered"**

Sing: "Angels, From the Realms of Glory" (p. 57)

• **Discuss: "Saints before the altar bending, watching long in hope and fear"**

• **Who was one of the saints watching for Jesus?**

Listen: The Magi were Gentiles. Do you remember what Simeon said about Gentile people? Simeon said that Jesus was the Savior for Jewish people and Gentile people. Gentiles did not know a lot about God or His plan to send Jesus. But when the Magi saw the bright star, they knew that a king from God was born. They lived far away from Jerusalem but they wanted to give gifts to the new king. When the Magi got to Jerusalem, they asked everyone where they could find the new king. The Jewish people should have known that the Messiah-King was born (Nu. 24:17). Why were the Jewish people not looking for the Messiah-King?

King Herod was not happy with the Magi's questions about a new king. King Herod asked the religious leaders where the Messiah-King was to be born. They knew the Messiah-King would be born in Bethlehem (Mi. 5:2). Did the religious leaders want to go to Bethlehem with the Magi? No.

The Jewish religious leaders knew what God's Word said about the Messiah-King. But they cared more about themselves more than about God. People can do religious things and not care about Jesus. Some can even celebrate Christmas and yet not think about Jesus. The religious leaders needed to stop pretending to know God and listen to what He wanted them to learn. They needed to believe the truth about Jesus and ask God to forgive their sins. Those who ask for God's forgiveness will be given the best gift ever. They will be forgiven of their sin. And they will be given life forever with God.

Truth: *God forgives anyone who believes the truth about Jesus.*

Discuss:

1. Who were the Magi and why did they want to see Jesus?

2. What did the religious leaders know about Jesus?

3. Why did the religious leaders not care about Jesus?

Memorize: Review–Luke 2:1-18

• Day 21—Summarize Luke 2:13-18 in your own words.

[13] And suddenly there was with the angel a multitude of the heavenly host praising God and saying, [14] "Glory to God in the highest, and on earth peace among those with whom he is pleased. [15] When the angels went away from them into heaven, the shepherds said to one another, "Let us go over to Bethlehem and see this thing that has happened, which the Lord has made known to us." [16] And they went with haste and found Mary and Joseph, and the baby lying in a manger. [17] And when they saw it, they made known the saying that had been told them concerning this child. [18] And all who heard it wondered at what the shepherds told them.

Sing: "Angels, From the Realms of Glory" (p. 57)

• Discuss: *"Sages leave your contemplations"*

• What are sages?

Listen: The Magi were so happy when King Herod said that they would find Jesus in Bethlehem. Herod pretended to be happy, but he was not. Herod wanted to find out when Jesus had been born. Why did Herod want to know this? Herod wanted to get rid of Jesus. He wanted to know when Jesus had been born. Herod pretended to want to go and worship Jesus too. But he was lying.

Herod was pretending to want to worship Jesus but he was angry. He did not want anyone other than himself to be king. And Herod was afraid. He was afraid that Jesus would take away his job and power. Herod was jealous. He wanted people to worship him, not Jesus. Herod started to think about how to kill Jesus (Mt. 2:16).

Herod did not have to stay angry, afraid, and jealous. God will forgive anyone of their sin if they ask Him. And God gives His Spirit to live in those who trust in Him. God's Spirit gives us the power to say "no" to sin (Rom. 8:9). But Herod did not want to believe the truth about Jesus. He did not ask God to forgive him. Herod kept his anger, fear, and jealousy. He did not love God. God warned the Magi not to go back to tell Herod where they found Jesus. And God warned Joseph to take Jesus and Mary far away to Egypt. Herod had evil plans (Mt. 2:13). But God kept Jesus safe.

Truth: God's plan for Jesus cannot be stopped.

Discuss:

1. Was everyone happy when Jesus was born?

2. What could Herod have done when he was angry, afraid and jealous?

3. How did God protect Jesus?

Memorize: Week 4–Luke 2:19 -20

• **Day 22—Memorize Luke 2:19; say verses 1-19**

¹⁹ But Mary treasured up all these things, pondering them in her heart.

• **Discuss: What does "ponder" mean?**

Sing: "Silent Night, Holy Night" (p. 59)

• **Discuss: *"with the angels, let us sing alleluias to our king"***

• **What is the difference between King Herod and King Jesus?**

Listen: Will you give any gifts this Christmas? What special gift might you give to someone you love? The Magi had special gifts for Jesus. They knew Jesus was a king sent by God. They brought Him gifts of incense, myrrh and gold. Why did the Magi bring incense? Incense smells like sweet perfume when it is burned. Incense was burned in the temple for the worship of God. The Magi wanted to worship Jesus. What does it mean to worship? It means to praise Jesus for who He is. The Magi did not know much about God or His Word but they believed what they knew. They worshiped Jesus as the Messiah-King that God promised to send. They were not pretending – they really did worship Jesus. How do we worship Jesus? We worship Jesus by praising Him for being our King.

What is myrrh? Myrrh is a mixture of spices. The best myrrh is very expensive. Myrrh was put on the body of a person after they had died. Why did the Magi bring myrrh? The Magi probably did not know that Jesus was going to die to take the punishment for our sin (Jn.12:1-8). But in giving myrrh to Jesus they worshiped Him for being the Savior. Jesus gave His life so we can be forgiven. Jesus is the Savior of every person who trusts in Him (Acts 10:43). How do we worship Jesus? We worship Jesus by praising Him for being our Savior.

Gold is a very special metal. It costs a lot of money to buy something that is made of gold. Rings and necklaces are often made of gold. Kings wear crowns made of gold. Why did the Magi want to give Jesus gold? They wanted to show Jesus how worthy He is to be worshiped. How do we worship Jesus? We worship Jesus by praising Him for being our Savior and King. Jesus is the only one worthy of our worship.

Truth: Jesus is our Savior and King.

Discuss:

1. Why did the Magi give gold to Jesus?

2. Why did the Magi bring incense and myrrh?

3. How will you worship Jesus?

Memorize: Week 4–Luke 2:19-20;

• **Day 23—Memorize Luke 2:20; say verses 1-20**

[19] *But Mary treasured up all these things, pondering them in her heart.* **[20] And the shepherds returned, glorifying and praising God for all they had heard and seen, as it had been told them.**

• **Discuss:** *"for all they had heard and seen, as it had been told them."*

Sing: "Angels, From the Realms of Glory" (p. 57)

• **Discuss: "Brighter visions beam afar"**

• **What brighter visions might the Magi have seen?**

Listen: Who will you give gifts to this Christmas? Will you give gifts to those you love? Will you give to friends who give gifts to you? Would you ever give an expensive gift to someone who did not love you? God gave us the most costly gift and best gift He could give. God gave us the gift of Jesus (1 Pet. 1:19). And God gave us the gift of Jesus even before we loved Him (Rom. 5:7-8).

God gives us many gifts to show His great love. He gives the gift of sunshine, rain, food, work, rest, family, and friends. But the gift of Jesus is the greatest gift of all. God's plan to send Jesus to earth means our sin does not have to keep us apart from God forever. God sent Jesus to live on earth because He loves you. God wants you to live with Him forever. God sent Jesus so we can have the gift of eternal life.

What is eternal life? Eternal life is living with God forever. Eternal life is given to everyone who believes. What are we to believe? We are to believe the truth about Jesus. Jesus is the way God planned for us to be forgiven and live with Him forever (Jn. 14:6). God has given you this gift, but have you taken it? Someone may give you a gift, but unless you take it, it is not really yours. It is the same with God's gift. To take God's gift means to thank Him for loving you so much that He sent Jesus to be your Savior. It means to ask God to forgive you. It is to ask God to help you obey Him and live for Him every day.

Truth: God gives the gift of eternal life to those who believe in Jesus.

Discuss:

1. What are some gifts that God has given to you?

2. Why is God's gift of Jesus the greatest gift of all?

3. What is eternal life?

Memorize: Week 4–Review Luke 2:19-20

• **Day 24—Summarize verses 19-20 in your own words.**

19 But Mary treasured up all these things, pondering them in her heart. 20 And the shepherds returned, glorifying and praising God for all they had heard and seen, as it had been told them.

Sing: "O Little Town of Bethlehem" (p. 58)

• **Discuss: *"The wondrous gift is given! So God imparts to human hearts the blessing of his heaven."***

• **What is the "wondrous gift"?**

Listen: Why do we celebrate Christmas? Christmas is the celebration of Jesus' birth. Why did Jesus come to earth? He came to give us a great gift. We did not have peace with God because of our sin. But Jesus took our punishment for sin so that we can have peace with God. When Jesus was born the angels sang, "Glory to God in the highest, and on earth peace to men on whom his favor rests." People who trust in Jesus have peace with God. Jesus gives us peace with God and the great gift of living forever with God—eternal life.

When Jesus was born God invited the shepherds and Magi to meet Him. God invited many other people to meet Jesus too, so they could know Him as their Savior and King. And God's invitation is for us today. God is inviting you to meet Jesus and to know Him as your Savior and King. To know Jesus is to trust in Him and want to live for Him. Is Jesus your Savior and King?

When we love Jesus we want others to know Him too. We want our family and friends to know how much God loves them. God wants us to tell others about His invitation to meet Jesus. Christmas is a good time to ask people, "Do you know why we celebrate Christmas?" Who will you talk to and ask this question? What will you tell a person who wants to know the answer to this question?

Truth: *Jesus came to give the gift of living forever with God.*

Discuss:

1. What keeps us from having peace with God?

2. What invitation does God give to us?

3. Who will you invite to meet Jesus?

Memorize: Week 4

• **Day 25—Review Luke 2:1-20**

Sing: "Hark! The Herald Angels Sing" (p. 56)

• **Discuss: "God and sinners reconciled"**

• **How did Jesus give us peace with God so that we can live with Him forever?**

SONG 1: "Hark! The Herald Angels Sing"

by charles wesley

1739

Hark! the herald angels sing
"Glory to the newborn King!
Peace on earth and mercy mild
God and sinners reconciled!"
Joyful, all ye nations rise
Join the triumph of the skies
With the angelic host proclaim:
"Christ is born in Bethlehem!"
Hark! the herald angels sing
"Glory to the newborn King"

Christ by highest heav'n adored
Christ the Everlasting Lord!
Late in time behold Him come
Offspring of the Virgin's womb
Veiled in flesh the Godhead see
Hail the Incarnate Deity
Pleased as man with men to dwell
Jesus, our Emmanuel
Hark! the herald angels sing
"Glory to the newborn King"

Hail the heav'n-born Prince of Peace!
Hail the Son of Righteousness!
Light and life to all He brings
Ris'n with healing in His wings
Mild He lays His glory by
Born that man no more may die
Born to raise the sons of earth
Born to give them second birth
Hark! the herald angels sing
"Glory to the newborn King"

SONG 2: "Angels, from the Realms of Glory"

by James Montgomery (1816)

Stanza 5&6 is from The Christmas Box, 1825

Angels from the realms of glory,
Wing your flight o'er all the earth;
Ye who sang creation's story
Now proclaim Messiah's birth.

Refrain

Come and worship, come and worship,
Worship Christ, the newborn King.

Shepherds, in the field abiding,
Watching o'er your flocks by night,
God with us is now residing;
Yonder shines the infant light:

Refrain

Sages, leave your contemplations,
Brighter visions beam afar;
Seek the great Desire of nations;
Ye have seen His natal star.

Refrain

Saints, before the altar bending,

Watching long in hope and fear;
Suddenly the Lord, descending,
In His temple shall appear.

Refrain

Sinners, wrung with true repentance,
Doomed for guilt to endless pains,
Justice now revokes the sentence,
Mercy calls you; break your chains.

Refrain

Though an Infant now we view Him,
He shall fill His Father's throne,
Gather all the nations to Him;
Every knee shall then bow down:

Refrain

All creation, join in praising
God, the Father, Spirit, Son,
Evermore your voices raising
To th'eternal Three in One.

Refrain

Song 3: "O Little Town of Bethlehem"

by Phillips Brooks

1868

O little town of Bethlehem
How still we see thee lie
Above thy deep and dreamless sleep
The silent stars go by
Yet in thy dark streets shineth
The everlasting Light
The hopes and fears of all the years
Are met in thee tonight.

For Christ is born of Mary
And gathered all above
While mortals sleep, the angels keep
Their watch of wondering love
O morning stars together
Proclaim the holy birth
And praises sing to God the King
And Peace to men on earth.

How silently, how silently
The wondrous gift is given!
So God imparts to human hearts
The blessings of His heaven.
No ear may hear His coming,
But in this world of sin,
Where meek souls will receive him still,
The dear Christ enters in.

O holy Child of Bethlehem
Descend to us, we pray
Cast out our sin and enter in
Be born to us today
We hear the Christmas angels
The great glad tidings tell
O come to us, abide with us
Our Lord Emmanuel.

Song 4: "Silent Night, Holy Night"

by poem written by Austrian priest called Joseph Mohr

1818

Silent night, holy night,

All is calm, all is bright

Round yon virgin mother and Child.

Holy Infant, so tender and mild,

Sleep in heavenly peace,

Sleep in heavenly peace.

Silent night, holy night,

Shepherds quake at the sight;

Glories stream from heaven afar,

Heavenly hosts sing Alleluia!

Christ the Savior is born,

Christ the Savior is born!

Silent night, holy night,

Son of God, love's pure light;

Radiant beams from Thy holy face

With the dawn of redeeming grace,

Jesus, Lord, at Thy birth,

Jesus, Lord, at Thy birth.

Silent night, holy night

Wondrous star, lend thy light;

With the angels let us sing,

Alleluia to our King;

Christ the Savior is born,

Christ the Savior is born!

About the Author

Barbara Reaoch is Bible Study Fellowship International's Director of children's programs. For nearly twenty years, she taught women's BSF classes in the U.S. and South Africa. Barbara also worked at the Rafiki Girl's Center in South Africa, teaching the Bible and life skills to young women. She has been married to Ron for over forty years; they have three grown children and four grandchildren.

Carol McCarty is a wife, mother, and grandmother. She was a high school biology and art teacher over a twenty-six year period. She has attended Bible Study Fellowship for eleven years and was a B.S.F. children's leader for four of those years. Carol is currently an artist specializing in pastels and acrylics. She and her husband reside in Coeur d'Alene, Idaho.